Women of the American West

Women of the American West

Liz Sonneborn

Franklin Watts
A Division of Scholastic Inc.
New York • Toronto • London • Auckland • Sydney
Mexico City • New Delhi • Hong Kong
Danbury, Connecticut

Note to readers: Definitions for words in **bold** can be found in the Glossary at the back of this book.

Photographs © 2005: Bridgeman Art Library International Ltd., London/New York: 44 (Edward Sheriff Curtis/The Stapleton Collection), 2 (Newell Convers Wyeth/Private Collection/Christie's Images); Colorado Historical Society: 36 (C-Auraria/Tom Noel Collection), 21 (F10489), 51 (F21400), 5 bottom (F33373), 41 (F33373), 33 (F3714/Green & Concannon), 13 (F3731), 46 (F50228/Charles Goodman), 38 (F5441/O. T. Davis), 11 (F6517); Corbis Images/Bettmann: 23; Getty Images: 26 (William Thomas Cain), cover, backcover ghost (Hulton Archive), 18 (MPI/Hutlton Archive); Kansas State Historical Society, Topeka, Kansas: 20, 25, 28, 30, 34, 42, 49; Montana Historical Society: 29 (O.C. Bundy), 22; North Wind Picture Archives: 6, 9; The South Dakota Art Museum, South Dakota State University: 5 top, 19 ("Fixing Fence", by Harvey Dunn); State Historical Society of North Dakota, A7182: 16; University of Southern California, Regional History Collections: 14.

The photo opposite the title page shows a pioneer family preparing to eat its evening meal on the trail West.

Library of Congress Cataloging-in-Publication Data

Sonneborn, Liz.
  Women of the American West / Liz Sonneborn.
    p. cm. — (Watts library)
  Includes bibliographical references and index.
  ISBN 0-531-12318-9
  1. Women pioneers—West (U.S.)—History—19th century—Juvenile literature. 2. Frontier and pioneer life—West (U.S.)—Juvenile literature. 3. West (U.S.)—History—19th century—Juvenile literature. 4. West (U.S.)—Social life and customs—19th century—Juvenile literature. I. Title. II. Series.
  F596.S715 2005
  978'.02'082—dc22   2005001468

Contents

The covered wagon of a homesteader family heading West with its belongings

Chapter One

Heading West

"We had lived in Springfield three years and were very happy and prosperous and the future looked bright," Martha Gay Masterson wrote of her youth in Missouri. Still in 1851, when Martha was thirteen, her father "got the Western fever. He talked about Oregon and the Columbia River . . . and wanted to go there."

By that time, many other Americans had also caught the "Western fever." Beginning in the 1840s, thousands of families left their homes and headed to what is now the western United States. Some wanted their share of the gold discovered in California. Others were looking for a warm, healthy climate. But most were like Martha's family. They wanted a plot of good, cheap western farmland they could call their own.

Leaving Home

The decision to go west was often made by the male head of the family. Sometimes, women were hesitant to uproot their families. But just as often, women were eager for adventure. One young **pioneer** named Mary Moore McLaughlin remembered her mother's enthusiasm: "[F]ather always said that whenever he wanted to move he had only to tell [M]other of his plans and she was ready and willing to go."

In the mid-nineteenth century, most pioneer families traveled west in **covered wagons.** But before heading out, they had to gather enough supplies for the trip. Men bought the wagons and the animals, usually oxen, to pull them. Women purchased or made nearly everything else. They had to sew clothing and wagon covers, buy cooking supplies, dip candles, and fix and pack food. It took months, sometimes years, to obtain everything needed.

For many women, the hardest part about going west was saying good-bye to friends and family. Although relatives often took the trip together, everyone left some loved ones behind. For Martha Gay Masterson, the "saddest parting of

Westward Ho!

Between 1841 and 1866, about 350,000 Americans moved west of the Mississippi River.

8

all" was her mother's final farewell to Martha's grandmother. The two women would never see each other again.

Women on the trail had many duties to keep them busy.

Trail Life

On the trail, pioneer women could sometimes steal a private moment. If there was room, they might sit in the wagon. There, they could quietly read letters from home or jot down notes in their diaries. But as soon as the wagons stopped for the evening, women were constantly busy.

Charlotte Stearns Pengra, who traveled west in 1853, kept a list of her many daily chores in her journal. One entry read: "I hung out what things were wet in the waggon, made griddle cakes, stewed berries and made tea for supper. After that was over made two loaves of bread stewed a pan of apples prepared potatoes and meat for breakfast, and mended a pair of pants." Not surprisingly, she ended the entry with two words—"pretty tired."

Women's biggest responsibility was preparing meals. While the men and children rested, women cooked over simple stoves or open fires, no matter how bad the weather was. An eighteen-year-old traveler named Esther Hannah wrote, "It is very trying on the patience to cook and bake on a little green wood fire with the smoke blowing in your eyes so as to blind you, and shivering with cold so as to make the teeth clatter."

To add a little variety to their meals, women often picked berries and onions growing wild near their campsites. A far less appealing chore was gathering fuel for the campfires. If tall grass or twigs were not available, they had to use chunks of manure, called chips, left behind by buffalo. Doing laundry was difficult as well. Women had to carry their families' dirty clothes to the nearest stream. There, they spent hours rubbing the fabric clean as their skin roasted in the hot sun.

Women also had to struggle to keep their children safe. The trail was full of dangers. A child could easily fall into a campfire or out of a wagon. Occasionally, children were crushed to death under a heavy wagon wheel.

Wagons West

A typical covered wagon and the oxen needed to pull it cost about $400, a large sum of money at the time.

There were no doctors on the trail, so mothers had to treat measles and other childhood diseases with homemade medicines. Women relied on each other to help with childbirth. Many women had babies on the way west. They usually took just one day of rest before their wagons continued over the trail.

This woman is cooking for her family over a simple stove, while dealing with the typical distractions of trail life, including children and animals.

Sorrows and Joys

The weather caused still more hardship. On the open **plains,** heavy rains and snowstorms could be terrifying. Amelia Stewart Knight wrote in her diary about a particularly fearsome lightning storm that killed two of her oxen. She said, "The wind was so high I thought it would tear the wagons to pieces."

Equally scary to many women were American Indians. Around the campfire, pioneers often told horrible stories of Indian attacks on women and children. Few of these tales were true, however. Many Indians who encountered western travelers just wanted to trade with them.

Homesickness also troubled pioneer women. Even when surrounded by fellow travelers, women often felt lonely when they thought of what they had left behind. Many tried to hide their feelings. Lavania Porter wrote that she sometimes wandered off alone to cry, "wishing myself back home with my friends."

Despite the trials of trail life, pioneer women had joyous moments. Many fell in love with the scenery they encountered. They wrote diary entries about colorful wildflowers and clear blue streams. For Elizabeth Cummings, the most stirring sight was the mountains of Utah: "Never have I imagined any thing like what I have seen . . . the most unearthly, weird, wild scenes."

Evenings around the campfire could also be fun. Once the day's work was done, travelers brought out fiddles and guitars. Everyone in the camp danced and sang. Women also treasured quieter moments, sharing stories and advice around the fire. Sitting with their trail friends, they marveled at how far they had come as they imagined with excitement what lay ahead.

Jessie Benton Frémont

13

A Western woman receiving official notice that she owns her homestead

Chapter Two

Farm Life

The final destination for many western pioneers was a **homestead.** A homestead was a plot of land on which a farming family could build a house and plant fields. Beginning in 1862, the U.S. government allowed a family to claim a homestead of 160 **acres** (68 hectares). The land was almost free if the family stayed on it for at least five years.

After months on the trail, women were thrilled when they finally reached their homesteads. But soon they saw

Land for Women

The Homestead Act of 1862 allowed women to own land for the first time in American history.

their hard work had just begun. A South Dakota pioneer named Katherine Kirk wrote, "With a sinking feeling I realized that I was entering a new kind of life, as rough and full of ups and downs as the road over which we traveled."

In many ways, pioneer women were well-prepared for homesteading. Life on the trail had taught them useful skills and lessons. They knew how to work hard. They had learned how to deal with any problems that came their way. And they were determined to succeed, no matter what.

Two women sit inside their tiny shack in Dakota Territory, decorated with as many of the comforts of home as they could bring west.

Building a Home

The first thing homesteaders did was build a house. Where trees were plentiful, they could construct sturdy homes from wooden planks and logs. But on the plains of the central United States, most homesteaders built sod houses, also called soddies. Made from bricks of dirt and grass, they were warm in the winter and cool in the summer. But with dirt walls and floors, they were hard to keep clean. Even worse, they leaked during rainstorms, making a muddy mess inside.

Women tried to make their soddies homey. They covered the floors with wooden boards and sometimes tacked up newspapers on the windows to make curtains. Many proudly displayed the few treasures they had brought from home. A piece of fine china on the table or a rocking chair in the corner made their soddies seem much more like a real home.

Once the railroad was built, trains brought tar paper, heavy paper coated with tar. Some pioneers used it to build their homes. These tiny paper-covered buildings were so **flimsy,** however, that a strong wind could knock them over.

A homesteading family's first house usually had only one small room. At night and during bad weather, the house was crowded with people. Farm families often had several other relatives living with them. For Rachel Bella Calof, of all the difficulties of being a homesteader, "the lack of privacy was the hardest to bear."

A Full House

On average, western farm women had ten children, although between three and four of them often did not survive past childhood.

17

Women's Work

Women spent most of the day in their cramped living quarters, working hard to keep their family clothed and fed. In addition to sewing and cooking, they had to make cheese, soap, cloth, and candles. There were usually no stores nearby where they could buy these goods.

While doing their housework, women also had to raise their children. All children, even the youngest, helped out with farmwork. It was a mother's responsibility to teach them how to clean the house, milk cows or goats, feed animals, gather wild plants, and carry water in from a nearby stream.

This illustration shows a typical pioneer farm cabin.

A homesteading couple repairs the fence surrounding its farm.

Men planted, plowed, and harvested the fields. But there was so much work to do that women often pitched in. For some women, this hard labor was their favorite part of homesteading. Carrie Dunn wrote of her homesteading mother's love of working outdoors: "She was a neat and efficient housewife, but repairing fences, searching for livestock or hunting were always legitimate excuses to take her out[side]."

Many women also spent their working hours making goods for sale. They grew vegetables and fruits to sell to neighbors. They also raised chickens for their eggs and made butter to earn extra cash. It often took years for a family to establish a successful farm. In the meantime, the money women made often kept their families from starving.

Butter for Sale

Some hardworking women produced as much as 100 pounds (45 kilograms) of butter a week.

A sewing circle in Kansas

Settling In

The first years on a homestead were usually the hardest. Living on isolated farms, homesteaders were not always sure they would survive. As more people moved West, they grew more confident. They enjoyed bigger harvests and built larger, more comfortable houses.

Each year, western farm families greeted new neighbors. As more people came west, towns grew up. Homesteaders could then get together for parties and other social occasions. Women often met for sewing circles. At these events, they visited with each other while sewing quilts and mending clothes.

With other farm families close by, women had more support in hard times. They helped one another give birth, nurse ill family members, and mourn the death of loved ones. But even with the aid of female friends, many homesteading women never felt secure. They resented the never-ending work. They hated the stifling summers and freezing winters. They lived in fear of violent storms and raging prairie fires. Some women gave up and returned east. A few were so overwhelmed that they lost their sanity.

Most farm women, however, rose to the challenges of the West. Their lives were often hard, but that only made them more proud of their accomplishments. Homesteader Elinore Pruitt Stewart spoke for many western women when she wrote, "I just love to experiment, to work, and to prove out things, so . . . 'roughing it' just suit[s] me."

This woman is working her field by horse-drawn plow, a difficult and exhausting job.

In Virginia City, Montana, women meet in their town's first church.

Chapter Three

Taming the West

When women pioneers first arrived in the West, they worked hard to build homes and farms. But once settled, they began to look beyond their families to the needs of their communities. There were few schools, churches, hospitals, and libraries. With the same energy they devoted to their homesteads, women, alongside men, set about creating these institutions near their new homes.

Women were particularly interested in establishing schools. They did not want their children growing up without an education. The first schools in the West were started by mothers, who taught their children at home. Over time, many took on their neighbors' children as students, perhaps charging their parents a small fee. One mother, Agnes Sengstacken, wrote, "My school teaching [was] quite a relaxation [from] my family and housework."

Pioneer Teachers

Women also worked together to construct permanent school buildings. Mabel Sharpe Beavers recalled how some women in her community "took up collections and bought rough lumber." With the students' help, they "built that school house with their own hands."

Children stand in front of their one-room sod schoolhouse in Kansas.

Once a town had a schoolhouse, its residents often hired a professional teacher. Most western teachers were educated in the East. Many were unmarried women. At the time, teaching was one of the only legal jobs that single women were allowed to hold.

About six hundred female teachers were sent west by the National Board of Popular Education. All board-approved teachers had to attend a six-week training session and promise to stay at their teaching posts for two years. For their work, they received a very low salary. Often, these teachers could not afford their own homes. Instead, they lived with a student's family, cleaning and cooking to earn their keep.

The teacher in this Kansas schoolhouse was likely unmarried and poorly paid.

Hard Work, Low Pay

In the West, female teachers were generally paid only half as much as male teachers.

The Western Classroom

Teaching in the West was also a challenge. Many school-houses were little more than shacks. Teachers had to work hard to fix up the cold, dirty buildings. While school was in session, they had to haul water for their students and protect them from wandering animals.

Angie Mitchell encountered an unusual problem teaching in the Arizona desert. One day, as she faced her class, she felt

Katherine Drexel

something tug at her skirt: "[T]here lying on my . . . skirt in a ray of sunlight was as hideous a reptile as I've ever seen." In time, Mitchell got used to the ugly lizard visiting her classroom. It spent many mornings sleeping on top of her desk.

Most western schoolhouses had one big room with about thirty students in many different grades. For example, one teacher in Ashland, Oregon, had twenty-eight students, ranging in age from five to twenty-nine. Discipline, especially with older students, was a common problem. Some teachers carried rulers so they could easily whack any student who got out of line.

When their two-year contract was up, some teachers packed their bags and headed back to the East. Some stayed, but quit teaching to become farmwives. A few, though, found they loved being teachers. As one western teacher said, "I like the West so much, and see so much need of teaching here, that I have no intention of ever going home to stay."

Katherine Drexel

In the late nineteenth century, many Catholic nuns traveled west to aid and educate Indian peoples. Among them was Katherine Drexel (1858–1955). Drexel grew up in a wealthy Pennsylvania family. Donating a fortune of about $20 million to various charities, she helped establish schools for Indian children on **reservations** throughout the West. In 2000, the Catholic Church granted Drexel sainthood, making her the second American-born saint in history.

Spreading Culture

Women in the West were not just interested in schools for their children. They wanted to help everyone in their communities improve their minds and spirits. For this reason, women formed clubs devoted to a wide variety of activities—from putting on plays to documenting local history to establishing scholarships for young men and women.

Many clubs raised funds to build churches. Most pioneer men and women were used to going to church every Sunday. They enjoyed the chance to talk with friends and listen to stirring sermons. For many, churchgoing was the highlight of their week. Pioneers also believed they had a moral responsibility to establish churches. As one Missouri woman complained, without church services, many men felt free to spend their Sundays on less uplifting activities, including "drinking, horse racing and gambling."

Western club women devoted themselves to many other worthy causes. The women of the Helena Improvement Society, for instance, worked to build parks and clean sidewalks in Helena, Montana. The Ladies' Hebrew Benevolent Society

Churches like this one were a welcome addition to any pioneer town.

28

in Los Angeles, California, cared for sick women among the city's Jewish residents. African American women in Kansas created an especially ambitious network of women's clubs. They focused on everything from instructing girls in needlework to providing child care for working mothers.

Later, many of the schools, hospitals, and other institutions created by western women were taken over by local governments. Some people forgot who started these institutions, but the women remembered. As a proud club woman in Dundas, Minnesota, recalled, "Those men believed they built [our] church, pointing it out with pride, [not] realiz[ing] it was the Ladies' Aid who really stemmed the tide."

Western women were active members of their local communities.

Working women in a New Mexico café

Chapter Four

Working Women

In the mid-nineteenth century, women were expected to stay at home, cooking and cleaning for their families. If they worked outside the home, it was usually in a family-run business. But these women were rarely paid for their work.

However, as towns in the West grew, so did the job opportunities for women. For the first time, many began to work for wages. Some just liked the independence of earning their own money. Most, though, worked for purely practical reasons. They had to earn a living to keep their families fed and clothed.

Women's Work

For many western women, working outside the home was much like working inside it. Their jobs involved doing household chores, such as cleaning, cooking, sewing, and washing clothes. Many young women worked as **domestics,** or servants. Parents often hired out their oldest daughters to add to the family's income. Domestics had to work very hard for little money. Emily French, a domestic in Colorado, complained that her boss was "crazy to ask me to do such a wash for such a price."

The pay was somewhat better for women working in western mining camps. Hoping to strike it rich, men set up these camps wherever gold or silver was discovered. Usually, they left their wives at home. Unaccustomed to doing housework, miners were happy to hire women to cook and clean for them.

At one Colorado camp, a former slave named Clara Brown charged fifty cents for each shirt she washed. She cleverly invested everything she earned in land. Within a few years, Brown had a fortune of $10,000, which would be worth about $140,000 today. She used her fortune to find the family that slavery had separated from her.

Keeping House

Women could earn even more by opening boardinghouses. For a fee, boardinghouse operators offered single men a room and three meals a day. Establishing a boardinghouse was easy. Libby Smith Collins remembered that her mother's boardinghouse in Denver, Colorado, was nothing more than a tent. Though her "only table . . . was a large stump," Collins's mother found "plenty who were satisfied to put up with the accommodations offered and pay . . . $16 per week for meals alone."

Often, a couple worked together to run a boardinghouse.

Clara Brown, former slave and savvy businesswoman

The husband dealt with customers and made household repairs. The wife did everything else, including cooking and cleaning, often for more than a dozen men. But even with their husbands' help, the job was too much for many women.

In a letter to her sister, one exhausted boardinghouse keeper in California looked forward to quitting and heading for the country after making some fast money: "I assure you I have to work mighty hard . . . it is nothing but gold, gold—no social feelings—and I want to get my part and go where my eyes can rest upon some green things."

Harvey Girls outside a Harvey hotel in Syracuse, Kansas

Finding Work

Women seeking work often moved to growing western towns. There, some found work in **saloons,** where they were paid to dance and keep company with the male customers. Life was often dangerous for saloon girls. Many were beaten or caught deadly diseases. Sheriffs sometimes threatened to arrest them unless they paid big bribes. Just the threat of jail was extremely frightening to saloon girls. Western courts generally gave women much longer sentences than they gave men.

Some women in these towns worked as waitresses, seam-stresses, shop clerks, and postal workers. Yet, many businesses were unwilling to hire women. Mrs. J. W. Likins discovered this when her husband became ill in 1868. Likins searched for

The Harvey Girls

Among the West's most famous working women were the Harvey Girls. They worked as waitresses for the Fred Harvey Hotels. The company recruited attractive, well-bred young women from the East. Job candidates were required to have "pleasant dispositions, good manners, and an eagerness for adventure." Harvey Girls received a monthly salary of about $18, plus room and board. Most took the job hoping for something more: the chance to build a new life in the West.

any job, with no success. Finally, she convinced a publisher in San Francisco, California, to hire her as a door-to-door saleswoman. Shy and reserved, Likins at first had trouble asking strangers to buy her wares. But as her selling skills improved, she earned enough to support her entire family.

Rather than waiting for someone else to hire them, many women started businesses of their own. For example, after Abigail Scott Duniway's husband was injured in a farming accident, she opened a successful millinery (hat shop) in Albany, Oregon, to support her family.

Edith and Ida Mary Ammons, two sisters in South Dakota, were even more ambitious. After establishing a homestead, they started a newspaper and opened a general store. They then taught themselves enough about the law to offer legal services to homesteaders. Like many other women, the Ammons sisters attributed their success to the independence the West offered them. As Edith Ammons wrote, "Its hardships were more than compensated for by its unshackled freedom."

A Fortune in Pies

In just a few years, one woman in California made enough money to retire by baking and selling 1,200 pies a week.

AK ERY

We
Use
Butter
In -
Our
Bread

BREAD

These women in Colorado were among the many women who carved their own place in a male-dominated society.

Chapter Five

In a "Man's World"

Men and women lived in very separate worlds in nineteenth-century America. Women usually stayed close to home, denied the chance to hold positions of authority beyond the family. But in the West, these boundaries sometimes broke down. Many western women began engaging in activities then considered unladylike—from driving cattle to practicing law to fighting for political causes. Either by choice or by necessity, these women dared to enter a "man's world" and make it their own.

Hard Labor

On family farms and ranches, women often performed heavy labor. Even though clearing land and branding cattle was considered men's work, women frequently helped out with these tasks. A few women took jobs as farmhands and laborers. In Montana, a former slave named Mary Fields was legendary for her physical strength. She made a living hauling goods in a horse-drawn wagon through all kinds of weather.

Sometimes, women ran their own farms. Many were widows who took over the family farm after their husbands'

These women are doing the hard work of branding cattle on a Colorado farm.

The Story of Mountain Charley

In 1846, Elsa Jane Guerin found herself in a tough situation. Her husband had just been murdered. Only sixteen years old, she was left to raise two children alone. But as a young woman, she doubted she could earn enough to take care of them. Guerin could think of only one way to save her family: She put on men's clothing and found a job as a cabin boy on a steamship.

For thirteen years, Guerin lived a man's life. She worked on ships and trains before heading to the mines of California and Colorado. She often thought about giving up her disguise. But aside from the money she earned as a man, she was hesitant to lose what she called "the freedom of my new character."

In 1859, however, her secret came out. Using the name Mountain Charley, she was running a saloon in Colorado. There, she tracked down her husband's killer and shot him. The man survived and, out of revenge, revealed she was a woman. Guerin then took off her men's clothing, married her **barkeep,** and returned to life as a woman.

death. But others chose farming as their profession. Among them was Harriet Strong. She became the first woman to join the Los Angeles Chamber of Commerce after establishing a prosperous business growing walnuts and pomegranates.

Other women sought their fortune as miners, panning for gold alongside rough and desperate men. Most women miners came away with little, but a few prospered. One Colorado woman found enough gold to buy seventeen mines. Another became the vice president of a mining company. In 1900, she claimed that mining could "be made to pay by any energetic woman who will pursue it in an intelligent way."

Pursuing a Profession

Jobs that required a college education were far out of reach for most nineteenth-century women. At the time, few colleges and universities would admit women. But most that did were located in the West. As a result, western women had a better chance of entering professions that required a college degree.

For some women, a love of the outdoors inspired them to pursue a career in science. Jeanne Carr became a botanist, a scientist who studies plants. She explored the western wilderness, hiking dangerous trails through the Yosemite Valley. Martha Maxwell was another well-known scientist. In the 1860s, she moved to Colorado, where she collected and stuffed animal specimens. Her exhibitions of animals made her famous across the United States.

Other western women were attracted to medicine. Most women learned basic first aid so they could nurse sick relatives. A few, though, sought more formal medical training. Many women of the Mormon religious faith, for example, studied nursing at Utah's Deseret Hospital.

A small number of women earned full medical degrees. Among them was Susan La Flesche. After graduating from The Women's Medical College in Philadelphia, Pennsylvania, she returned home to the Omaha Indian reservation in Nebraska. A member of the Omaha tribe, she spent many years serving her people.

Like medical schools, most law schools barred women. But at least one western woman, Clara Foltz, fought this policy.

Annie Oakley

Perhaps the best-known western woman of the nineteenth century was Annie Oakley. At twenty-five, Oakley was so skilled at shooting guns that she was invited to join Buffalo Bill's Wild West Show. As a star of this popular traveling show, Oakley wore a cowgirl outfit and performed sharpshooting tricks for cheering crowds. In one trick, Oakley rode through the arena on horseback, shooting three rifles to shatter six glass balls thrown in the air.

Martha Maxwell, with two of her specimens

While raising five children, she trained herself in the law. Still, the University of California law school refused to admit her. Representing herself, she sued the university and won the right to study there.

Frances Willard

Testing the Boundaries

In the nineteenth century, American society taught women to stay quiet about political matters. They were not even allowed to vote. But several causes drew western women into the nearly all-male world of politics.

Temperance was a particularly important issue for women. The **temperance movement** was an effort to persuade people to stop drinking alcohol. Many women thought temperance would protect wives and children from men who became abusive when they were drunk. Still, some women were afraid they would be called unladylike if they joined the movement. One temperance organization in San Jose, California, encouraged women to speak out anyway. One of its pamphlets declared, "Young ladies, throw away all timidity. . . . Think not what people will say, but come boldly to the front and God will reward you."

A few women grew so bold that they started to campaign for suffrage—the right to vote. Among them was Frances Willard. In 1883, she traveled throughout the West, encouraging women to become more politically active. She declared that women needed the vote as "a weapon for the protection of the home." Largely because of Willard and other female activists, the West led the way toward women's suffrage. By the end of the nineteenth century, four western states—Wyoming, Utah, Colorado, and Idaho—had granted women the right to vote.

Getting the Vote

In 1869, American women in Wyoming Territory became the first women in the country to be granted the right to vote.

The lives of American Indians, like these in Montana, were forever altered by the increased movement of non-Indians to the West.

Chapter Six

Natives and Newcomers

Every woman who moved to the West faced challenges. But in many ways, western life was especially hard for women who were American Indians, Hispanics, African Americans, and recent immigrants from foreign lands. Most had to carve out a new life in an unfamiliar place. And as ethnic and racial minorities, they also had to cope with hostile neighbors who looked down on them and their ways of life.

A Navajo Indian woman in Utah weaves a blanket using the techniques of her ancestors.

The First Western Women

Dozens of Indian tribes lived in the West long before Americans arrived there. In fact, some tribes had been there for thousands of years. Each group had its own customs, but all western Indian women worked hard to clothe, feed, and house their loved ones. Some farmed small plots of land. Others skinned the buffalo their husbands killed. Many made objects, such as pots and baskets, that their families used every day. For their labor, Indian women earned the respect of other tribe members.

With the arrival of non-Indians in their lands, Indian women's lives changed forever. As American settlers took over their lands, some tribes fought back. Indian women grieved when their husbands and sons were killed in battle. A few women also lost their lives in these bloody conflicts. Eventually, the U.S. government forced many Indian peoples onto reservations. There, government officials tried to make Indian women live as non-Indian women did. They were forced to give up the traditions that in the past had filled their lives with meaning.

American values also influenced western Hispanics. These people were the descendants of Spanish explorers and settlers who first came to the West in the sixteenth century. Before the arrival of Americans in the region, Hispanic women could inherit land. Some became rich landowners. Doña Vicente Sepùlveda, for instance, owned a large ranch in California, where she was well known as a clever and successful businesswoman. But once Hispanic women were subject to American law, they were no longer allowed to own property. Eventually, wealthy Hispanic women like Sepùlveda lost all their land and money.

Poor Hispanics suffered as well. Once Hispanic women on small farms prided themselves on taking good care of their families. Tending gardens of melons, pumpkins, and corn, they grew much of the food their husbands and children ate. They also brought money into their households by raising goats and chickens. But after Americans took over western lands, many Hispanic women took jobs outside their homes as domestics and cooks.

Searching for Freedom

A few African American women arrived in the West in the early nineteenth century. Most headed for California and other places where gold and silver were discovered. Clara Brown, for example, became a washerwoman in a Colorado mining town. She earned enough money to purchase freedom for thirty-four relatives, and she paid for them to come west by wagon train.

Only in the 1870s, however, did a large number of African Americans head west. Most were former slaves who had been freed after the Civil War (1861–1865). They were drawn to the American West for two reasons. They wanted to escape the South, where they had been treated badly by whites. They also wanted the chance to farm their own land.

Mary Ellen Pleasant

One of the most important figures in nineteenth-century San Francisco was Mary Ellen Pleasant (1814–1904). Born in Pennsylvania, Pleasant moved west during the California gold rush. Slowly, she built up a fortune through smart investments. An African American, Pleasant used much of her money to help other blacks freed from slavery. She also funded several important lawsuits, including an 1863 case that allowed African Americans to testify in California courts.

For most, the destination was Kansas. About 20,000 African Americans flooded into this state in the 1870s. They founded several all-black towns, including Nicodemus. These African American settlers were called **Exodusters.**

Most Exodusters were desperately poor. They lived in sod houses, while struggling to start farms. But the soil was so bad that some found it impossible to make a living. To survive, men took odd jobs and women worked as domestics. Some African American families gave up on Kansas and moved back to the South. But others stayed, no matter how hard they had to work to survive.

The townspeople of Nicodemus, Kansas, in 1885

Among them was Willianna Hickman, who arrived in Kansas in 1878. When she first saw her sod house, she cried. But as she later remembered, "Days, weeks, months, and years passed and I became reconciled to my home." Proud of her pioneer struggles, Hickman recalled, "We improved the farm and lived there for nearly twenty years."

To a New Land

Just as the Exodusters were eager to leave the South, many Europeans headed to the West to escape terrible lives in their homelands. In the late nineteenth century, many people in Ireland, Germany, Italy, Norway, and Sweden were very poor. Some chose to **immigrate** to the United States, hoping to settle on western homesteads.

The journey west was long and exhausting. European immigrants first had to survive the journey across the Atlantic Ocean in ships that were overcrowded and unsanitary. Then they had to travel hundreds of miles overland by wagon, boat, or train. Once immigrants reached their homesteads, they found themselves in a strange land with customs they did not understand. Even worse, many did not speak English. Unable to talk to nearby settlers, many felt isolated. In time, however, the lives of European women improved. As they learned more about American ways, they began to blend in with their American-born neighbors.

Immigrants from China, however, had a far more difficult time adapting to their new surroundings. In the mid-nineteenth century, many Chinese men came to the West to mine for gold or silver, or to work on the railroad. Some were joined by their wives. Because the ways of Chinese immigrants were unfamiliar, whites looked on them with suspicion. Fearing violence, Chinese women rarely left their neighborhoods or even their homes. Still, many of those women played a central role in helping relatives build successful family businesses.

During the nineteenth century, the West attracted women of many different backgrounds from all over the world. The region held out to them the promise of a new and better life. For many, it was a promise kept. In the West, women found a wild landscape, full of both danger and beauty. Living on the land and working the soil, many nourished their families and their dreams. In the West, women also discovered new

These women, and many others, found a new life waiting for them in the West.

freedoms. Old rules about what was considered ladylike behavior often no longer applied. The demands of living in this largely unsettled land dared them to make up new rules. Surviving untold hardships, many rose to the challenge to become women of the West.

Timeline

1836	Missionaries Narcissa Whitman and Eliza Spalding are the first non-Indian women to cross the Rocky Mountains
1841	The Bidwell party becomes the first wagon train to travel overland to Oregon and California
1845	John C. Frémont's *Report of the Exploring Expedition to the Rocky Mountains,* written with his wife Jessie, inspires thousands of Americans go west
1847–1858	The National Board of Popular Education sends hundreds of female teachers to work in western schools
1848	January: Gold is discovered in California; February: The end of the Mexican War brings much of the American West under the control of the United States
1861–1865	The American Civil War is fought
1862	The U.S. Congress passes the Homestead Act, which allows heads of families (including women) to claim 160 acres (68 hectares) of western land
1869	Wyoming Territory grants women the right to vote
1870	American women in Utah Territory vote in an election for the first time

1874	The Women's Christian Temperance Union is founded
1879	About 20,000 southern African Americans move to Kansas
1882	The U.S. Congress passes the Chinese Exclusion Act, which restricts the immigration of Chinese men and women to the United States
1885	Sharpshooter Annie Oakley joins Buffalo Bill's Wild West Show
1889	Susan La Flesche becomes the first female American Indian to graduate from medical school
1890	The U.S. Bureau of the Census declares there is no longer any "free land" available in the West

Glossary

acre—an area equal to 4,840 square yards (4,046 square meters); many family farms in the American West were 160 acres (68 hectares)

barkeep—bartender

covered wagon—a large horse-drawn cart with a canvas roof used by settlers to travel west on overland trails in the mid-nineteenth century

domestic—a household servant

Exodusters—African-Americans who settled in Kansas during the 1870s

flimsy—thin or weak

homestead—the house and nearby land occupied by a western farm family

immigrate—to leave one's country and settle permanently in another country

pioneer—a person who settles in unfamiliar territory

plains—a large area of flat, treeless land, such as the Great Plains of the central United States

reservation—an area of land set aside for the use of an American Indian group

saloon—a place where alcoholic drinks are sold

temperance movement—an organized effort to persuade people not to drink alcohol

To Find Out More

Books
Fiction:

Gregory, Kristiana. *Across the Wide and Lonesome Prairie: The Oregon Trail Diary of Hattie Campbell, 1847.* New York: Scholastic, 1997.

Gregory, Kristiana. *Seeds of Hope: The Gold Rush Diary of Susanna Fairchild.* New York: Scholastic, 2001.

Nonfiction:

Alter, Judy. *Extraordinary Women of the American West.* Danbury, Conn.: Children's Press, 1999.

Katz, William Loren. *Black Women of the Old West.* New York: Atheneum, 1995.

Ketchum, Liza. *Into a New Country: Eight Remarkable Women of the West.* Boston: Little Brown, 2000.

Sonneborn, Liz. *The American West.* New York: Scholastic, 2002.

Stefoff, Rebecca. *Women Pioneers.* New York: Facts On File, 1995.

Organizations and Online Sites

National Cowgirl Museum and Hall of Fame
1720 Gendy Street
Fort Worth, TX 76107
http://www.cowgirl.net
The site provides a thorough introduction to the only museum dedicated to honoring the pioneering spirit of the women of the American West.

History of the American West

http://memory.loc.gov/ammem/award97/codhtml/hawphome.html

This Library of Congress site features a searchable database with more than 30,000 images dealing with the history of the American West.

New Perspectives on the West

http://www.pbs.org/weta/thewest

This site, set up by the Public Broadcasting Service, offers a wealth of information on people, places, and events in Western history.

WestWeb

http://www.library.csi.cuny.edu/westweb/pages/women.html

WestWeb's "Women in the West" page provides links to biographies, photographs, and selections from diaries.

A Note on Sources

In recent years, a number of historians have done pioneering work in the study of western women, attacking old stereotypes while revealing the wide range of roles women played in western history. As an overview to these reevaluations, I found particularly helpful *Frontier Women: The Trans-Mississippi West, 1840–1880* by Julie Roy Jeffrey (Hill & Wang, 1979); *A Place to Grow: Women in the American West* by Glenda Riley (Harlan Davidson, 1992); and *Uncommon Common Women: Ordinary Lives of the West* by Anne M. Butler and Ona Siporin (Utah State University Press, 1996). Written for young adults, Harriet Sigerman's *Land of Many Hands: Women in the American West* (Oxford University Press, 1997) is another solid introduction to current research on women in the West. Among general sources, *Pioneer Women: The Lives of Women on the Frontier* by Linda Peavy and Ursula Smith (Smithmark, 1996) is noteworthy for its wealth of interesting photographs.

Several essay collections were useful in writing this book. They include *The Women's West*, edited by Susan Armitage and Elizabeth Jameson (University of Oklahoma Press, 1987), and *So Much to Be Done: Women Settlers on the Mining and Ranching Frontier*, edited by Ruth B. Moynihan, Susan Armitage, and Christiane Fischer Dichamp (University of Nebraska Press, 1990). I also enjoyed the lively biographies in *By Grit & Grace: Eleven Women Who Shaped the American West*, edited by Glenda Riley and Richard W. Etulain (Fulcrum, 1997).

Lillian Schlissel's *Women's Diaries of the Westward Journey* (Schocken Books, 1982) is an excellent source of information on western women's experiences told in their own words. I also highly recommend *The Western Women's Reader*, edited by Schlissel and Catherine Lavender (Perennial, 2000), for its large and thoughtful selection of primary sources.

For general questions about western history, I consulted two reference works that make especially good use of recent scholarship in the area: *The New Encyclopedia of the American West*, edited by Howard R. Lamar (rev. ed., Yale University Press, 1998); and *The Oxford History of the American West*, edited by Clyde A. Milner, Carol A. O'Connor, and Martha A. Sandweiss (Oxford University Press, 1994).

—*Liz Sonneborn*

Index

Numbers in *italics* indicate illustrations.

About the Author

Liz Sonneborn is a writer and an editor living in Brooklyn, New York. A graduate of Swarthmore College, she has written more than fifty books for children and adults, including *The American West, A to Z of American Women in the Performing Arts,* and *The New York Public Library's Amazing Native American History,* winner of a 2000 Parent's Choice Award.